The Phoenix Paradigm

The Phoenix Paradigm

Designing Your Business for the 21st Century

A Strategic Guide
To Outsourcing

Cheryl R. Frank

Published in the United States by:
Blink Ink Press, Inc.

ISBN: 978-0-6151-9026-6

Book Design by:
Gary Weiss

For information about bulk purchases
and special discounts, please contact:
GO Global at 877-462-7680
or Arlene@goglobalbpo.com.

.

To Joshua,

*for the power
of his imagination
and love.*

TABLE OF CONTENTS

About The Author

Cheryl Robin Frank (Cheryl) grew up in Chicago at the dawn of the civil rights and women's liberation era. It was before the term "global warming" was in the lexicon, when winter was still winter. Cheryl was a thoughtful child, and as she matured, she saw the world in a different light, perhaps the effects of those long months of frosty nights, followed by hot, humid summer days.

At Georgetown University, she started to think, "If you're wearing a necktie to work every day, nine times out of ten, it is cutting off the circulation to your brain." Still, she did what she was told and became a CPA, went to law school, then topped off her law degree with an LLM. She took the standard professional path of working for the government in the U.S. Treasury Office of Chief Counsel, in a division that dealt with Tax Litigation and Civil/Criminal Tax Shelters. Cheryl's "left brain" thinking took over and she became a process specialist, working the system.

After four years, she became a partner in a respectable Washington, DC law firm specializing in mergers and acquisitions. Three hundred mergers and acquisitions later, Cheryl decided it was time to break out on her own. The entrepreneurial genes from her father helped thrust her to the surface.

Realizing she needed to be the architect of her own destiny, Cheryl started her own law firm in 1993. It grew to 14 associates and support staff. Representing over 3,000 clients with tax and business problems, she learned that CEOs' lack of attention to the bottom line and unwillingness to change put each and every one of her clients on the brink of collapse. Those that were willing to listen to Cheryl and follow her direction turned around their businesses. They are millions of dollars richer today.

Cheryl successfully shifted away from law and into real estate investment, and business management and development. She continues to improve and reinvent businesses, mentoring CEOs and entrepreneurs. Her long time law clients refuse to relocate to new counsel, and her loyalty has allowed them to keep coming back for direction and advice from Cheryl, their proven guru.

After almost three decades of giving advice and overseeing implementation of her strategies, Cheryl has developed a proven methodology for turning around any business. Her system has been trademarked *Panoply Pro®*. She has given Deconsulta, Inc. the exclusive rights to use this proven formula for the business community.

To assist in the implementation of a company's Panoply Pro personalized plan, Cheryl created a new company, GO Global, the nation's foremost business opportunity provider.

With the onset of computer technology and the utility of the Internet, Cheryl recognized that the outsourcing model could be a superior way to conduct and deliver business processes in an economical manner. Combining her business acumen with outsourcing, she founded GO Global as a BPO provider specializing in finance and accounting services for the mid-market.

Cheryl can be reached via email at cheryl@goglobalbpo.com. With GO Global, a world of ideas is as close as your phone.

Professional credentials:

Cheryl R. Frank received her Bachelor of Science degree from Georgetown University, summa cum laude, in 1978, and her Juris Doctor, with honors, from the University of Miami School of Law in 1981. She earned a Master of Law in Taxation from Georgetown University, with honors, in 1984. She is a member of the bars of the District of Columbia, Florida and Maryland.

*Change is the constant, the signal
for rebirth, the egg of the phoenix.*
CHRISTINA BALDWIN

Preface

The *Phoenix Paradigm* is all about recharging your business by making positive changes, one of those through outsourcing. When properly implemented, the outsourcing process can be one of the most effective methods to renew and revitalize your business. If you are one of the many CEOs and business owners struggling with the day-to-day operations of running a business, you are probably worried about cash flow, industry competition, and profit growth. We have used the Phoenix bird as our symbol because it has the ability to survive and be reborn. A good CEO, who can survive in today's fast changing and complex world economy, needs to consistently revise the old paradigms of doing business and adapt to new ones to excel.

Outsourcing has become one of the most predominant business models of our times, as a result of new technologies that have compressed the world. Some people are out-and-out opposed to outsourcing. Others find it difficult to understand. Yet outsourcing is increasing at an astonishing rate. When it is properly implemented, outsourcing can become an incredibly cost-effective business management tool that can literally change the entire organization into a stripped down, money-generating machine. This happens because essential, but ordinary business processes get disentangled from the core-functions, which are the profit centers and heart of any viable business.

Not long ago, outsourcing meant call centers in India. Gradually CEOs at legendary multinational companies realized that it was just as feasible to outsource well beyond just these call centers, into research and development (R&D), human resource administration, and finance and accounting. The motivation to outsource is quite simple -- reducing costs, access to a strong labor pool, and adding value.

This book was written on the conviction that outsourcing is a strategic business tool, that it is beginning to be recognized by the small and mid-market enterprise sector, and that the implementation of shifting non-core functions to a third party expert is being perfected and professionalized. We acknowledge, however, that making the decision to outsource does not come easy, that it sometimes means letting go of some employees, and past traditions as well.

Imagine, though, a well-organized workplace with the most cutting-edge information technology…that provides effortless billing and collecting accounts receivable with none of the headaches…a daily updated accounting system which provides accurate and timely data at the touch of a button. No more worries about cash flow fluctuations… no more surprises, because data gives you a clear picture of what's coming up. Imagine, experts that manage all of your back-office processes while cutting costs up to 50%...no more employee turnover disrupting business…running your business with key indicators at your fingertips from anywhere in the world…having real time access to statistical trends in your business and industry, monthly, so you can spot issues and resolve them before they become problems… increasing bottom line net profit and the value of your business on its sale or acquisition…tax planning throughout the year to save money on your taxes…and your company at the top of its industry.

After more than 26 years in law, tax, business management and accounting, I believe we have entered the next frontier by incorporating all of the digital technologies that allow companies to utilize the best and most competent professionals no matter where they are located.

You may be searching for a new vision, a new direction, and a new platform on which to grow their business. This book intends to assist you in moving your business to the next level and position your company for success in the 21st century.

Introduction

The first goal of business is to make money. Every other reason is a distant second. But the rules of the game are changing and succeeding in today's marketplace has become increasingly complex; 80% of new businesses fail in the first two years and 96% fail by the tenth year. As a CEO, you have to make strategic decisions through a long range telescope with a wide lens. The landscape is rapidly expanding, and a good leader looks beyond the ordinary horizon to find new vistas of opportunity. A great leader must have a five-year plan during which the business is reshaped, perhaps reinvented, to fit the shifting global landscape. If you study the most innovative companies in the U.S., you will find that they are constantly looking for new business innovations and new ways to serve their customers. Such outstanding companies range from tech giants like Google and Apple to consumer product standouts, such as Johnson & Johnson and General Mills, to financial conglomerates Bank of America and Citigroup. All of these companies are well positioned for growth year after year, because they share many of these common characteristics:

- Have a vision of the future
- Creativity and ingenuity
- Flexible and able to quickly change to keep up with competitors
- Mindful of reducing overhead to conserve capital
- Attentive to the bottom line net profit
- Concentrate on the core competency (what the company does that makes money) and delegate the rest to the experts!
- Place high priority on the people who make the money (rainmakers)

Great business leaders continually assess new opportunities to advance against their rivals and outpace them. One of these opportunities is through outsourcing where non-core business functions, such as information technology (IT), human resources, and payroll, are performed at a lower cost and with greater efficiency and enlarged knowledge base by a specialized third party contractor. Today, enterprises of every size are choosing to outsource many of their non-core business functions to these specialists.

Through several business models, opportunities for outsourcing are becoming financially beneficial for small and medium-sized enterprises (SMEs) with limited back-office employees, which can benefit from turning over their administrative functions, accounting, and data processing to third party providers. Savvy executives recognize that the smoother and more efficient the wheels turn, the more productive and profitable the organization can be. Companies bogged down in the old ways of running businesses will lose value and will fail to survive. To thrive in today's highly competitive markets, companies have to act and react at superfast levels, so the leaner and more nimble the organization, the more they can win against an increasingly competitive and knowledgeable marketplace.

With my extensive background in law, tax and accounting, I have a thorough knowledge of the substantial amount of resources that are necessary to devote to non-core transactional processing. From 1980 to 1984, I worked in the Chief Counsel's office of the Treasury Department, I was a partner in a major law firm in Washington, DC, and then staffed and operated my own businesses for almost two decades. Through these experiences, I realized how much money and time is wasted on administrative tasks and more precisely "business processes."

In working with thousands of small to medium-sized enterprises from 1993 to the present, I saw how companies are mismanaged, wasting millions of dollars each year, because they do not know how to address the juggernaut of having to manage administrative personnel. Mismanagement will always result in business failure regardless of how unique the product/concept or how well positioned it is in the marketplace. By the time we were brought in, it was often too late to fix the problem. If the CEO had streamlined the information flow to allow quicker and more precise decision-making, business collapse could have been prevented in most cases.

One of the reasons I established GO Global is to help other companies streamline their organizations so they can improve their bottom line, hence, increase the value of their company and succeed.

Through *Panopy Pro,* my accounting and financial methodology, GO Global is pioneering the way in business process outsourcing (BPO) for small and mid-sized enterprises. Any company with more than five back office employees can achieve significant benefits and reinvent the way they run their businesses. We believe that "garbage in...garbage out" is dragging down small and medium-sized companies and suffocating their economic growth. In many cases where we are brought in to consult, we suggest that their business and accounting systems be redesigned. Often, hardware is outdated and other IT capabilities are obsolete. This guide is about how we propose to implement a new business strategy utilizing the newest technologies and the ability to outsource to the most competent professionals, wherever they are!

Happy reading!

Cheryl R. Frank
CEO
GoGlobal
www.goglobalbpo.com

ONE

Global Outsourcing: A Paradigm Shift
The Path to Outsourcing

Progress is impossible without change,
and those who cannot change
their minds cannot change anything.

GEORGE BERNARD SHAW

In the last decade, we have all benefited and been challenged by the incredible advances of computer technology, wireless telecommunications, and the exponential growth and utility of the World Wide Web. Thomas Friedman wrote in his bestselling book, *The World is Flat*, "The Windows-enabled PC and Apple computers made it possible for people to create their own content from their desktops in digital form. Advances in telecom made it possible for people to disseminate their own digital content in many new ways." Yes, technology has flattened the world enabling companies to capitalize on talent in every corner of the world... spending less and getting more. Most small to mid-market companies, however, have not taken advantage of all this new flat world has to offer.

Outsourcing is by no means an original concept, although the term was expanded from the word "sourcing," which refers to the act of transferring work and responsibilities to someone else. Managers are constantly delegating or sourcing work to other staff members who have time to do it faster and better. Every minute that a manager spends on administrative tasks takes away from the time he can spend on his real work. The practice goes back to the caveman days when we think that different tribes divided labor and exchanged the byproducts, often delegating tasks to those who performed them most proficiently.

In the 1960s and '70s, airplane transportation and long distance telecommunications enabled manufacturers to produce goods in the Far East where cheap labor was available in Japan, Taiwan, and Hong Kong. As a result, offshore manufacturing closed hundreds of textile and apparel factories in the U.S., particularly in the Northeast and in the South -- while clothing and footwear has become more affordable to the mass market.

In much the same way, new inventions and technologies have opened the road to the outsourcing of services and business processes. The World Wide Web, browser technology, email, and advanced software have made outsourcing of office based tasks possible. Beginning in the 1990s, large multinational companies began to go overseas to employ technical workers, and later, knowledge workers, because the salaries were less than half of what comparable workers in the U.S. earn. Not only was labor cheaper, but the workers were highly skilled and motivated, bringing a fresh eye to innovation.

With the Internet providing ready access to resources and knowledge, corporate thinkers started to focus more on core competencies to innovate and broaden their markets. For example, Colgate Palmolive outsourced all of their back office functions and now concentrates solely on product development. They began to realize how an organization can access external talent and expertise, without owning it or supporting it internally.

The combination of new technologies and applications, the renewed focus on core competencies to expand innovation, and the cost savings factor led to the spread of outsourcing models. Today, outsourcing companies innovate in technology, service solutions, and business processes.

Outsourcing initiatives have evolved from short-term projects to high-level business strategies that enable companies to increase revenues and profits in the competitive global marketplace.

Outsourcing is now the norm for almost every multinational company, including Microsoft, GE, Proctor & Gamble, Citigroup, and Aviva, the fifth largest insurance company, to name only a few. Most of the airlines outsource, as well as big retail companies. Dun & Bradstreet estimates that outsourcing is now a US$4 trillion a year industry. According to industry experts, 25% of the typical executive budget is outsourced, and projected to grow to 34% by the end of 2007.

Small and medium-sized enterprises (SMEs) are catching up with the giants. The benefits of outsourcing are clearly about much more than cost, and really about harnessing the global knowledge bank. Executives, who have been challenged more and more to increase margins consistently and over time, as well as to better position the business in the marketplace, know full well that they must streamline non-core business processes to survive and deliver the best possible product or service to their customers at a competitive price.

> *Never stop asking yourself,*
> *"What is our business?"*
>
> PETER F. DRUCKER

Technology, the bane of our existence ...

One more factor that has driven the need to outsource is increased sophistication of IT. Computer technology is a double-edged sword. It has empowered business and society, but has also made everything more complicated. We live in a world of wireless wizardry, ubiquitous laptops and PCs, and high maintenance office machines.

While these technical advances have enhanced our productivity, the office has become more complex and frustrating to work in because essentially it is still driven by paper documents, file cabinets, and office leases -- and lots of administrative staff to manage -- driving executive decision-makers to think about alternative business models to get the job done.

Accounting and data processing, for example, is a typical administrative function in any business. Though it is essential to the successful long term viability of the business, the activity does not generate revenue. It requires competent and trained, detail-oriented staff, office space, telephones, updated computer systems and accounting software, and all of it has to be maintained, repaired, and managed. Guess who does that in many mid-market companies… you guessed it…the CEO or top management. You think they have better things to do with their time?

Employee theft and inadequate hiring practices are another management problem that won't go away. Here are some of the facts:

- One-third of all employees steal from their employers, according to the Department of Commerce.
- A study by the University of Florida in 2002 estimates that employee theft represents $15 billion in U.S. business losses.
- 30% of business failures are due to poor hiring practices. Annual losses generated by poor hires, absenteeism, drug abuse, and theft amount to $75 million per year. (U.S. Department of Commerce-Atlanta Business Chronicle.)
- Small businesses with 100 or fewer employees are the most vulnerable.

It's no wonder, then, that outsourcing business processes has evolved into a strategic management tool that can take the pain out of back-office activities and put the plus sign back on the bottom line. CFOs and CEOs in the SME sector are getting the message that outsourcing, whether nearshore or offshore, is not just for the big guys. It has become the cornerstone of a paradigm shift in the way small and medium-sized enterprises will be run.

4

Characteristics of the new outsourcing model and business strategy for SMEs:

- Many business processes that were usually done internally, such as human resources, data processing, and accounting, are now being outsourced. They are essential functions but they are not your core competencies.

- Outsourcing has become more strategic in nature. It's become a management tool, and is much more than a cost-savings measure.

- Outsourcing has gone offshore and nearshore, even into emerging countries.

- Communications between companies and their outsourcing vendors has changed.

- Relationships between companies and their outsourcing providers are being reshaped through a consultative strategic joint venture approach.

- Outsourcing has become a profession and the professionals are developing standards and accreditation programs under the auspices of the International Association of Outsourcing Professionals (IAOP).

Key Issues to Consider in any Strategic Decision to Outsource

1. Outsource business functions that do not have to be done internally so you can focus on your core competency and grow your business.

2. Outsource specialized skills, such as finance and accounting or graphic design, that are necessary, but not core to your business.

3. Outsource rote tasks, such as data entry, that can be done by trained personnel more efficiently and more economically outside the U.S.

4. Outsource finance and accounting to a specialist in those areas. Many times a business can not find competently trained people in their geographic area to perform these functions, but other countries have many competently trained employees with those particular skill sets.

5. Outsource a portion of a certain function as a backup system and to spread risk.

6. Communicate regularly with your outsource provider.

7. Make sure that your outsource provider has security in place and backup systems.

8. Negotiate and select the right outsourcing model to achieve your business objectives. Not all outsourcing is the same! Not all models will achieve the intended results. Use a consultant to assist you if you are not sure!

Although jobs are lost to outsourcing or to offshoring or to new technologies, new jobs are also created in small companies that you can't see. This is happening because the global pie is growing larger -- because more people have more income to spend. America's knowledge workers have more competition but the market has expanded and become more complex. So it should turn out to be a win-win for America and the Far East. There will be, however, a shifting of jobs horizontally.

THOMAS FRIEDMAN
The World Is Flat

Is Outsourcing Really Hurting the U.S. Economy?

Before we go any further, let's talk about the effect of outsourcing on American labor. Outsourcing regularly gets a bad rap on the grounds that it shifts certain jobs away from Americans. The practice is used as a political football to garner support from workers that have lost their jobs to lower paid foreign personnel. This is basically the same scenario as when manufacturing went overseas. But that's what it is...a bad rap.

Outsourcing frees up money to ultimately create new jobs. On a macroeconomic level, outsourcing expands markets, and when we expand markets, we create wealth and spending power. A business model that helps raise the socioeconomic level of an emerging country and puts money in the peoples' pockets to buy imported products, like jeans and baby clothes, has the ability to benefit the entire planet. What goes around comes around.

Here is an example: if a worker in Guatemala is hired and trained to perform data processing work, he or she now has increased buying power, which often translates into purchases of American goods. Multiply this by millions of workers overseas and that translates into a great deal of spending. In a fair and open trading system, those dollars sent outside the U.S. for outsourcing will come right back to the U.S. purchasing our goods and services.

Workers that do lose their jobs can be shifted into new lines of work, sometimes for the better or trained to perform in core areas of the company. Employees who embrace the increasing globalization of the economy stand to reap big rewards!

What did the Bad Witch say to the Good Witch?
"They gave my job to someone in India.
Now I'm going to Beauty School."

TWO

Understanding Business Processes and BPO
What is this thing called BPO?

Identify functions in your organizations that could be outsourced. Make plans to outsource these functions and to monitor performance and quality.

PETER F. DRUCKER

Offshore BPO has been in the news since 2002. Business processes refer to back-office functions, including data processing and administrative operations, which are considered non-core activities. BPO combines two powerful business tools -- business process management and outsourcing. Most large organizations are comprised of departments that handle non-critical, but necessary, activities, such as sales processing, data entry, customer service, accounts payable, and accounting.

Let's take a look at a few different industries to understand core activities or "core competencies" compared to non-core activities, which are back office business processes:

For example, in the publishing industry, editorial content is a core competency, really the heartbeat of the organization. Advertising sales is a core competency, too, because it generates the revenue that allows the publication to operate. Business processes include circulation management, accounting and financial management, administrative functions, and payroll.

In the manufacturing industry, the core activity of the business pertains to product design and fabrication, whether it be steel, lighting fixtures, or shoes. Sales and marketing are vital to revenue generation. Back-office functions or business processes include transactional operations such as accounts payable and receivable, payroll and human resources, and sales inventory.

The core competency of a medical practice is the delivery of patient care. The business itself requires many back-office administrative functions, such as medical insurance claims processing, patient information management, and billing.

Each of these industries has customers/clients/patients. All of them have and need data processing and accounting functions. But they don't need these functions inside their business. If they outsource these functions, opportunity and success awaits.

BPO on the rise

In May 2005, David L. Margulius wrote in *InfoWorld* magazine that BPO is the next outsourcing wave.

The critical question here is: How can BPO be implemented for SMEs with up to 300 back-office employees?

The BPO provider and the enterprise develop a strategic cooperative, which allows the shifting of back-office functions to the BPO provider. BPO is the process by which this is accomplished.

The key to outsourcing is a systematic approach to the transition. If the right steps are taken and followed to the letter, then successful implementation will generate additional profitability and add value to the enterprise. (Please refer to Chapter Eight.)

Typical BPO functions to be outsourced include:

- Billing and Accounts Receivable
- Sales order processing
- Customer invoicing
- Accounts payable processing and payment
- Maintaining accounting systems and bookkeeping
- Generating trial balance and general ledgers
- Bank account reconciliations
- Preparation of financial statements: income statements, balances sheets, and cash flow statements
- Data entry
- Claims processing

Basic technology has launched the offshore BPO as a fundamental business solution. The challenge now is to make that solution as seamless as possible in order for the company to boost productivity and profitability.

Jagdish Dalal, an outsourcing expert, refers to the tipping point for offshore BPO, as "it will become a 'must do' strategy and not a 'may consider' one. There will be a technology foundation, process innovation, standards, benchmarks, and best practices and offshore BPO will be just another globalization tool."

Outsourcing of typical BPO functions is the most practical and strategic means to alleviate "garbage in…garbage out"-- creating a more flexible company, positioned for growth.

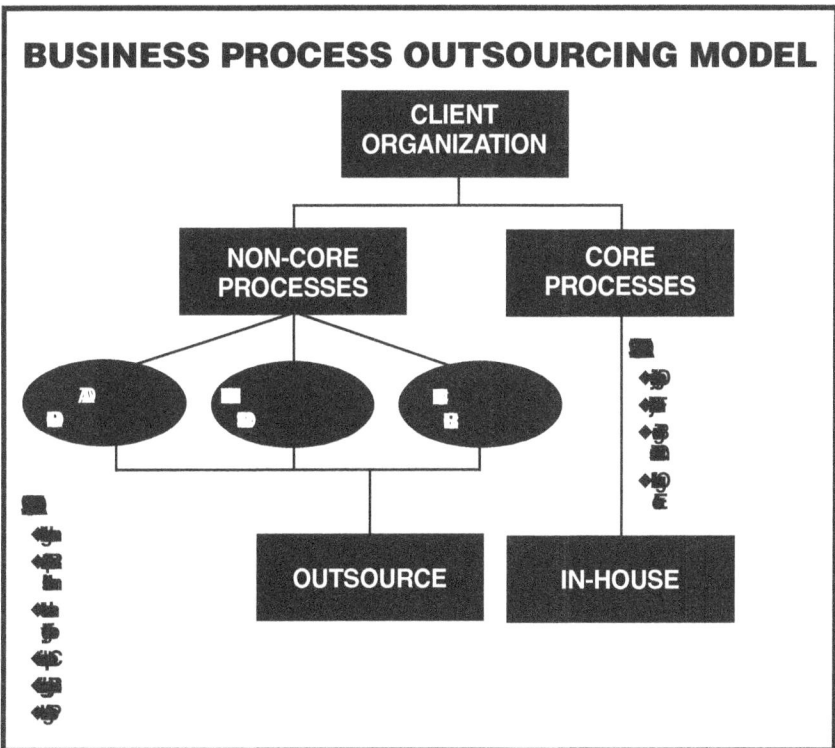

BUSINESS PROCESS OUTSOURCING MODEL

Industries likely to outsource

Insurance
- Data processing
- Claims processing
- Customer Relationship Management (CRM)

Publishing
- Customer invoicing
- General accounting and bookkeeping
- Subscription/circulation management

Non-profit
- General accounting and bookkeeping
- Donor list management
- Membership
- Receipting

Manufacturing
- General accounting and finance
- Research and development
- Inventory data processing
- Cost accounting

Real estate and construction
- General accounting and finance
- Rent rolls and tenant management
- Construction industry billing and costing

14 Benefits of Outsourcing

- Allows more time and energy to develop core competencies and increases ability to compete in marketplace.
- Reduces capital expenditures.
- Reduces investments in fixed assets.
- Adds time for management team that can be spent on mission critical issues.
- Increases control of operating costs, both fixed and variable.
- Improves speed of information and response time.
- Solves technology issues.
- Reduces IT obsolescence and associated risks.
- Allows the expert in the field to train and hire the right workers.
- Minimizes employee lawsuits.
- Minimizes bad hiring decisions.
- Minimizes expensive office space to house workers.
- Minimizes employee benefits or employment taxes.
- Reduces risk of employee theft or embezzlement.

THREE

Three Universal Outsourcing Models
Captive, Custom, and Temp

We must become the change we want to see.

MAHATMA GANDHI

The outsourcing of technology started in the late 1990s when companies such as General Electric discovered the potential of India. Others, including Microsoft, Dell, American Express, and IBM, soon followed. At first, they outsourced software development and IT services, but soon they were thinking, "Hey, why don't we peel off our customer call centers, claims processing, and human resources to India and the Philippines."

Over the last decade, several outsourcing models have evolved that are the most prominent, as described herein:

Model 1: Captive Center

This model is called "captive" because a Fortune 500 company will actually set up an entire operation offshore to perform business processes in a country where wages are lower and talent is plentiful. To implement the outsourcing process, a consultant plays a key role in making the transition. An experienced consultant will guide the company on business processes that should be outsourced, where they will set up a facility, and how the transition will take place. A Director of Outsourcing is hired to act as Chief Operating Officer for the newly established facility. This is a highly responsible position to oversee the offshore facility. Generally, such an executive can earn about $750,000/year. The captive model involves the actual construction or leasing of an offshore facility, hiring and training people, and establishing and operating a branch or subsidiary of the company overseas.

For example, Hewlett Packard shifted over 1,000 customer service jobs from Florida to the HP Center that they opened in India. Oracle also moved about 2,000 jobs to its captive center in India.

India has become the premier remote processing center of the world because of its relatively low labor costs and highly skilled, computer-literate labor force. Many of the largest corporations in the world, including IBM, Microsoft, Motorola, General Electric, American Express, and Citibank, have established "captive" centers in Bangalore, the high-tech capital of India. It is here that many business processes are conducted, including customer service, software development, and claims processing centers. But India is not the only place that excels in providing processing centers.

These captive centers can cost up to $10-15 million to set up and implement so the barrier to investment is high. Companies with back offices of less than 300 employees will not obtain financial return so other models are becoming more common in the mid-market.

Model 2: Custom Provider

A relatively new model provides customized outsourcing solutions for small and medium-sized enterprises (SMEs). A consulting company may be hired to assist in planning and implementing the transition to outsourcing. The provider will hire and train skilled workers dedicated to a specific client and business process, such as accounts payable, data processing, or financial statement generation. The provider will professionally train and recruit specific employees with a defined skill set to work offshore for the U.S. based company client.

There are two distinct variations of this model -- one, with a US-based company contract that offshores; the second, a contract with a foreign company, known as direct offshoring.

Model 3: "Temp Agency"

The "temp agency" outsourcing model is when a provider takes over in the same way as a temp or personnel agency. The firm provides employees to perform work for a significantly smaller fee, usually in India or China where workers receive lower wages than in the U.S. Generally, it is a small business owner or entrepreneur that contracts for a single service. For example, a physician or healthcare provider will pay for the processing of medical claims. A magazine may contract out its data input, such as subscriber or advertising list management. A service company that takes phone calls can hire a call center. The client will contract for a number of hours. The outsourcing provider usually has teams, but the teams handle multiple clients; they are not dedicated to one client organization.

In the SME sector, the key is in the planning and the migration of the business processes. Consultant and client team up to develop a "white board" of activities that make up each process. As part of the BPO process, the system is often reinvented to allow additional efficiency. Process analysis and workflow mapping form the basis for planning the outsourcing arrangement. Costs and performance levels are developed, quantifying the measures of success and tracking it.

There are a multitude of variations in contract terms that can be individually negotiated by the parties.

' WHO'S GOING TO TELL HIM HE'S BEEN OUTSOURCED ? '

FOUR

Trends in Outsourcing

The great business process invasion

Hell, there are no rules here --
we're trying to accomplish something.
THOMAS A. EDISON

Outsourcing has become a deeply entrenched business strategy that is rapidly maturing and evolving to deliver unique business value well beyond the original idea of cost reduction, according to a report from the International Association of Outsourcing Professionals (IAOP). Organizations are rethinking their place on the global landscape and incorporating outsourcing as a strategic long-term management tool. For many companies, the challenge is deciding what functions should be outsourced, selecting the most appropriate providers, and learning to work in concert with these providers to achieve the maximum long-term benefits for the company. As this pattern is established, outsourcing will move from a cost-driven, customer-supplier model to a full-fledged partnership or joint venture with the provider. They will work together to maximize the growth and profitability of the company.

Basic facts about current outsourcing trends:

- SMEs are gradually moving toward outsourcing to reduce costs and increase efficiency. Resistance is declining among mid-market companies that recognize an opportunity to add value.
- Socially responsible - According to the International Association of Outsourcing Professionals (IAOP), outsourcing increasingly will be recognized for the value it brings to communities around the globe.

- Faster Offshore Growth - major countries where services are outsourced are: India, China, and Canada.
- Emerging Countries Gain as BPO Destinations - Philippines, China, Brazil, Russia and Eastern Europe, some Central American countries, such as Costa Rica Guatemala, and Panama.
- The Gartner Group says that by 2010 about 30% of Fortune 500 enterprises will outsource to three or more different countries, from less than 10% in mid-2007.

Outsourcing professionals are working together to raise the standards of this growing industry. They are studying ways to establish professional guidelines and accreditation so that the practice of outsourcing will become increasingly professional and successful. Underperforming outsourcing relationships will be able to follow professional guidelines to step up their game and make it a win-win for the client company.

Near or far…work around the clock

Outsourcing does not necessarily mean offshore. Some McDonald's franchisees and JetBlue Airlines source out specific functions right here in the U.S. When you order a Big Mac through the drive-through, the order-taker may be at a call center in Colorado Springs. When you make an airline reservation on JetBlue, you may be talking to a stay-at-home Mom or Dad in Salt Lake City, Utah.

While India is best known as the premier IT outsourcing destination, a labor shortage is imminent. Many other global locations have become attractive, including Eastern Europe and China where research and development centers are flourishing, as well as call centers and BPO providers. Central America and Mexico are fast becoming visible as desirable nearshore centers for data processing and administrative functions.

One of the best advantages of offshoring is the benefit of large numbers of skilled employees. Accounting and financial activities can be performed overnight in Guatemala and data returned the following morning to clients in Miami and Chicago, for instance. Business operations that are tied into a global network can function 24/7. This speeds up time to process information and decisions can be made before it is too late. Invoicing and collections can be expedited to increase cash flow.

FIVE

Outsourcing Business Processes

Garbage in…garbage out

Drowning in data, yet starved of information.

RUTH STANAT

in *The Intelligent Organization*

Among all the general and administrative functions that a company deals with, data processing, finance and accounting are most likely to be outsourced. Findings by the Everest Research Institute revealed that 77 percent of such contracts have elements of offshore delivery. In other words, these functions are increasingly being outsourced.

Why does it make so much sense to outsource these activities? First, accounting is an essential business function that requires ongoing attention with the processing of data and information. Much of the work is highly detailed, entailing accurate data entry, reporting, and mechanical calculations. It is not, however, critical to the management of the core business. Crunching numbers and having solid financial records are necessary, but the function does not produce revenue. Secondly, good technical people are hard to find and expensive to hire in the U.S. Management should not waste time or the company's money on implementation and maintenance of non-core functions.

The repetitive nature of data processing and accounting tasks make this discipline an ideal function to source out, providing that the process is set up by an experienced provider/consultant in a collaborative relationship with the client. Once the system is in place, and expertly implemented, a well trained professional can routinely handle it. Planning and transition are explained elsewhere in this manual. Bear in mind that the implementation of the outsourcing process is of utmost importance.

Once we get from A to Z, one of the major benefits of outsourcing data processing and accounting is actually alleviating the burden of running a highly labor-intensive department. Besides significant cost savings, you can realize these direct benefits:

1. Improved management focus
2. Reduction in error rates on input
3. Reduced operating costs for office space, office supplies, and employee benefits
4. Access to global talent
5. Innovation

Net Profit the Goal

Outsourcing is likely to improve your net profit as well. It behooves every business to keep a close eye on its profits, which are eaten away quickly by steep and increasing overhead. In fact, the true health of any company can be gauged by its bottom line. BPO enhances the health of a business when savings are passed along to customers or reinvested into other areas of operations. Ultimately, streamlined business processes will increase the value of the business and make the company more attractive for acquisition and growth in its industry.

Jack Be Nimble, Jack Be Quick

As better Web-based applications are designed and introduced for SMEs, BPO will be even easier and less expensive...meaning, less worry about equipment and down servers, and constant software upgrades. Security will be greatly enhanced.

More small and medium-sized companies will be able to apply the outsourcing model to become more flexible. CEOs will be able to focus on strengthening core competencies and increasing value, and in so doing, position effectively for growth and exit.

Remember that investors nowadays are looking for companies that are lean and light, not high overhead companies with excessive fixed costs. The most desirable businesses are those generating revenues that can show clear-cut net profit and solid core competencies. Buyers do not want to acquire companies that are weighted down by hard assets, such as expensive high maintenance equipment used for non-core back-office functions, which can be outsourced for nickels on the dollar.

Exit Planning

Exit strategies have changed. Investors no longer want businesses with the trappings of office space and hard assets. Companies that buy other companies are looking for value, derived from a powerful core competency. Take PayPal, for example, a company that is basically an online pay service. When eBay acquired PayPal, it was because of its pay online business model, a perfect adjunct to its own online auction business. eBay was buying a methodology, not office leases or copy machines.

CEOs can create value by creating a flexible organization, not by having lots of equipment on their balance sheets. They need to focus on their cash flow and control overhead, so they can increase growth and create value. This will serve the CEO well during the inevitable down business cycles.

25

SIX

Barriers to Outsourcing
Pitfalls and Promises

I not only use all the brains that I have,
but all that I can borrow.

WOODROW WILSON

Many companies fear change. Certainly, changes as transformational as outsourcing come with risk. There are many decisions to make about what functions to outsource, where to outsource, and which provider matches your needs the best. Client and provider are entering into a type of marriage and after the honeymoon is over, there are always issues that must be resolved to obtain the maximum benefit out of the relationship.

Some of the negative feelings that can harm the relationship are based on:

- Fear of loss of control
- Activities and processes are perceived as too critical to be outsourced
- Perceived loss of flexibility
- Negative customer, employee, and community reactions
- Dependence on provider once function has been outsourced

There are also external factors that can affect the delivery of benefits. The key to successful outsourcing is sound planning, good communications, and hard work. The outsourcing consultant has to effectively direct the process and help in establishing an alliance between the company and the provider.

It is always best to set realistic expectations and to put them in writing. Choose the right functions to outsource as a starting point. Negotiate a balanced relationship that offers sustainable benefits for both customer and provider. Be prepared for the potential impacts on the organization and manage them. It can be done successfully!

Pitfalls and Promises (Solutions):

1. **LACK OF COMMITMENT AT THE TOP** - this is the biggest reason why promising situations fail to materialize or to work out. The commitment to a successful outsourcing initiative requires executive involvement and perseverance to resolve business problems. Many business owners do not even understand what their own companies' processes entail. Executives need to take a serious look at their business, including core competencies, competition, cost structure, growth strategies, and potential areas that would benefit from outsourcing. Change comes from the top!

2. **OUTSOURCING BROKEN BUSINESS PROCESSES** - don't outsource until you fix it first. Outsourcing is not intended to be a quick fix for core problems that endanger the business, such as inflated cost structures or obsolete technologies and inefficient processes. These issues must be fixed before the work is migrated.

3. **MISUNDERSTANDING OF OUTSOURCING METHOD-OLOGIES** - outsourcing is not a passing fancy. It is a complex business strategy with a life cycle. Adhere to a careful, well thought out transition plan to get it right.

4. **MISHANDLED TRANSITION** - schedule a sufficient time period to carefully transition those functions you identify for outsourcing; map out workflows with as much detail

as possible. Management must understand the long-term ramifications of the shift and convey the message to every level of the organization.

5. FAILURE TO ASSIGN THE BEST AND BRIGHTEST INSIDERS TO INTERFACE WITH THE OUTSOURCING TEAM - Identify high-performing internal people with a big picture frame of reference. It could be the COO, the head of IT, or the marketing director. These individuals should have good instincts and understanding about the corporate culture, marketplace, and business processes and systems.

6. POOR PLANNING, IMPROBABLE EXPECTATIONS - choose the opportunities for outsourcing that have the highest probability of delivering the intended results. Ask: what is going to be outsourced? When is it going to be outsourced? Who will be impacted? What plans are in place to mitigate the impact on those affected?

7. RUSHING THROUGH THE OUTSOURCING PROCESS - take each phase of the implementation in a disciplined manner. These steps are the foundation of the outsourcing program.

8. THE WRONG PROVIDERS - choose providers with expertise in the business process you want to outsource; do your homework and ask questions.

9. AN UNDERDEVELOPED RELATIONSHIP PLAN CAN SPELL DISASTER - design a relationship between the enterprise and the provider that offers long term sustainable benefits to both. There should be a relationship management plan that includes: descriptions of the outsourcing effort, a list of key stakeholders, schedule of responsibilities and

activities, and the roles of each of the players involved. Performance measurements, work products, required skills and knowledge should be spelled out.

10. LACK OF A CLEAR-CUT COMMUNICATIONS PLAN - outsourcing is a paradigm shift in the way a business will operate. Start on a firm note by preparing a comprehensive communication plan that positively articulates the purpose of the outsourcing initiative to your stakeholders. Include benchmarks to guide the business processes that will be outsourced and when.

SEVEN

How to Know When to Outsource
Getting on the Bandwagon

*The hardest thing in life is to know
which bridge to cross and which to burn.*

DAVID RUSSELL

Nobody says that outsourcing is easy or a quick fix to existing problems, but nothing worth having is easy. Many CEOs and their chief officers have their eye on outsourcing, but resist going through the process, because of the logistics and transition period. Sometimes, the business is really hurting and bankruptcy is even possible, yet they keep putting off the change until it is too late. SMEs in particular are accustomed to hands-on management, so there is an inflated fear of loss of control. In fact, the reverse is true. In many cases the management team will have more control as the business is streamlined and they will have real time access to relevant data needed to make quick transitions and to be really in control, versus the illusion of control. **CEO's can work at their business and stop working in their business. They can work smarter not harder.**

Examples:

(1) *A family-owned property management company in Maryland was tempted to change over to an outsourcing provider to free themselves of maintaining rent rolls and outdated accounting systems.*

(2) *The co-owner of a small beauty salon chain in Florida with 52 employees could no longer cope with the amount of bookkeeping he himself supervised each week.*

Both of these companies were afraid to give up control. They perceived that no one could do the administrative processes better than they could. The property management owners did not want to become dependent on an outside provider because they were so used to running a closely held, family-owned business. As for the salon owner, he decided to downsize. He sold his share of the business to his partner and bought a smaller salon that was easy enough for one person to manage.

You may think your company is operating fine and you have positive cash flow and profits. But if your company is not running at full speed and is inefficient, you should analyze the situation.

Ask yourself these questions:

- Is your business showing a profit?
- Are your sales growing year after year?
- Are your businesses processes operating smoothly?
- Do you need to add more qualified workers?
- How do you spend your time?

Studies show that most financial executives spend 50% to 70% of their time on the processing of transactions and reporting data. Many of the tasks are nothing more than input and output of data that a computer-literate individual properly trained can master. It doesn't take a CFO to handle accounts payable and receivable or even do financial projections. Outsourcing enables key officers to focus on strategic planning and high level core business development issues.

Are you spending too much time on managing administrative functions?

HOW FINANCIAL EXECUTIVES SPEND THEIR TIME

Transactions Processing and Oversight	25%
Accounting and Finance Functions	27%
Control and Risk Management	26%
Strategic Activities	22%

Four Best Reasons to Outsource

1. The primary reason for outsourcing is to reduce both labor and overhead costs. Unless you grow a business carefully, you will have insufficient cash flow and be inflexible to change. The less overhead you have, the more nimble the business is and that itself creates value.

2. The second most cited reason is the freeing up of time for executives to focus more completely on company resources and core activities that generate revenue. Resources include people, physical assets and intellectual property, and the core elements of operations. Several multinational growth companies that outsource are Microsoft, Proctor and Gamble, and Starbucks. By outsourcing back-office functions, they are able to better concentrate on product development and marketing. These activities are the heartbeat of a company and provide a unique competitive advantage.

3. The third most cited reason is to achieve a more variable cost structure. Outsourcing allows the company to manage down periods better because the company worries less about fixed costs such as office space and other large overhead expenditures. Rather than have relatively fixed investments and hard assets in its internal operation, the company shifts to a more on-demand business model. Many industries have for years adopted this practice to not only improve their bottom line, but to make business less structurally complex and therefore easier to manage. The on-demand business model reduces the cost of operations by enabling the company to adjust expenses in response to changes in the marketplace.

4. The fourth reason is to access skills not readily available locally. Talent is everywhere and the nature of today's technology enables companies to find the unique talent they might need in India, Guatemala, or Nebraska.

Check List for Change

Outsourcing your back-office functions can pay off substantially in relatively short order. The potential to reduce overhead costs is great as the business reduces salaries and employee benefits, as well as other ancillary costs, such as leasing of space, utilities, and purchases of computers and telecommunication related expenses.

SMEs should consider outsourcing back-office functions when some of these circumstances exist:

- When a company employs five or more back-office workers.
- When your net profit is less than you projected or below industry standard or you are over budget.
- When a significant amount of a CEO or CFO's time is spent managing and administrating back-office employees.
- When your back-office costs exceed 10% of revenues.
- When the turnover rate of back-office staff is more than 5% annually. Training and recruiting costs can drain your bottom line and waste management's time!
- When every time an employee leaves, you spend too much time searching for qualified replacements and pay recruiters large upfront fees.
- When computer systems become obsolete and software outdated, it may be the right time to shift to an experienced outsourcing provider with these systems currently in place.
- When the company is lagging behind its industry peers evidenced by published industry standards.
- When you do not get timely and accurate monthly profit/loss statements and financial statements, you are unable to manage your business effectively.
- When the data you are getting just is not correct!
- When a recession hits the U.S. economy it is time to get lean and cut costs!
- When the CEO and other top officers take frequent fishing trips and have contacted headhunters!

EIGHT

Implementing the Outsourcing Process

Take two aspirins and call your consultant

*I like to tell people that all of our products
and business will go through three phases.
There's vision, patience, and execution.*

STEVE BALLMER

Implementation is the most important aspect of the success of outsourcing. For each and every client, a consultative approach is the key to successful execution. The process starts by assessing and planning the needs of the client organization to determine if and how outsourcing might benefit the company's bottom line.

The issue to address is simply: What functions are costing too much money to run in-house, and beyond that, causing headaches for management? For example, let's suppose the company employs 35 back-office employees at a cost of $1.5 million per year in salaries and benefits to do accounting. Things are still not running smoothly, however, with delays in the processing of data and invoicing, among other problems. Then wouldn't the business do better to spend $850,000 annually for an expert that concentrates solely on accounting and data entry, one that can fix the problem and cut the costs in half?

To quantify the answer, sit down with a consultant and conduct a strategic analysis of the company's business processes to decide what to outsource and the best way to outsource.

An experienced consultant in process mapping works with the client organization to illustrate which tasks can be outsourced in isolation and which tasks need to be bundled. The map will show which functions are stand-alone and which are interdependent. For example, in the case of accounting, a bundle might include data entry, billing, and invoicing. Preparation of financial statements could be separate, but might also be part of the bundle.

During the assessment and planning phase, careful consideration should be given to metrics, the statement of work (SOW), and the service level agreement (SLA). Otherwise, it's like going into battle without battle plans. Don't expect to win at outsourcing without thorough planning and defining metrics. Choose metrics that are reasonable, easy to follow, and provide sufficient detail so they are subject to analysis.

Metrics helps an organization evaluate how the operating principles are being conducted by providing measures to show the level of compliance to each item. Here's where consistency is an important factor to ensure a high level of compliance. Each metric must be specified in detail, collected, and then interpreted throughout the project. For example, if the provider has been retained to manage accounts receivable, metrics may be set up to quantify collection ratios, frequency of customer contact, and the process to notify the client of uncollectible cases to be sent to the attorney. In the case of bookkeeping, the metrics may relate to the timeliness of data input or the parameters for defining error rates.

Statement of Work (SOW)

An SOW is an agreement that spells out the scope of work and the details of the project. It specifies the functions being supported, the type of work being performed, the deliverables, and the roles of each party in the effort. Always create an SOW that is detailed and understandable to both provider and client organization, especially insofar as the responsibilities of each and the deliverables that will be produced.

Service Level Agreement (SLA)

The SLA is one of the key elements of the outsourcing contract and must clearly reflect the expectations of the client organization over the life of the agreement. The document defines the parameters by which the work will be performed and judged.

SLAs should be attached to each specific SOW that corresponds with each project. Each major project defined in the SOW is assigned a performance criterion in the SLA. The SLA stipulates criteria such as: (1) volume of work to be completed within a given time frame, (2) acceptable response time for actions, and (3) quality requirements and measures of efficiency with lack of errors.

The performance criteria for each work assignment is described using metrics, which are selected to provide an accurate measure of performance, agreed upon by both the provider and client.

Service Level Agreement (SLA): What to Ask the Outsourcing Provider

Before you sign any contract, here are some questions you should ask the BPO provider:

1. **Which service levels will you measure?**
   There should be parallel incentives for outsourcer and client. For example, a fixed-price deal gives incentive to the outsourcer to cut corners, whereas the SLA should focus on quality.

2. **What will you measure for each service level?**
   Each service level should be precisely defined.

3. **How will you measure?**
   Put into place a process for measuring performance, such as user satisfaction surveys or key indicators, such as number of customers or net profit per sale.

4. **What is the measurement period?**
   Common intervals are monthly or quarterly. Find out if it covers 24/7 or 9-to-5.

continued next page

37

5. **How are results reported?**
   The SLA should define exactly what information will appear in performance reports.

6. **At what level will you perform?**
   The answer here is meaningful when you know what will be measured and how. An SLA can include both minimum and target service levels.

7. **Will service levels change over time?**
   Long-term, large-scale agreements can specify that service levels should increase over time and how increased fees will be charged.

8. **Should the SLA include bonuses?**
   Bonuses for exceptional service levels are acceptable and encourage a spirit of partnership toward the achievement of mutual goals.

9. **If service levels are not met, when does this result in termination for cause?**
   Agreements can be terminated for cause if there is a material breach of service that is severe. To avoid this possibility, make the SLA very detailed.

10. **What is a key to the success of the SLA?**
    You never want to outsource a problem. Get your house in order before you outsource and identify your business objectives and what you are trying to achieve.

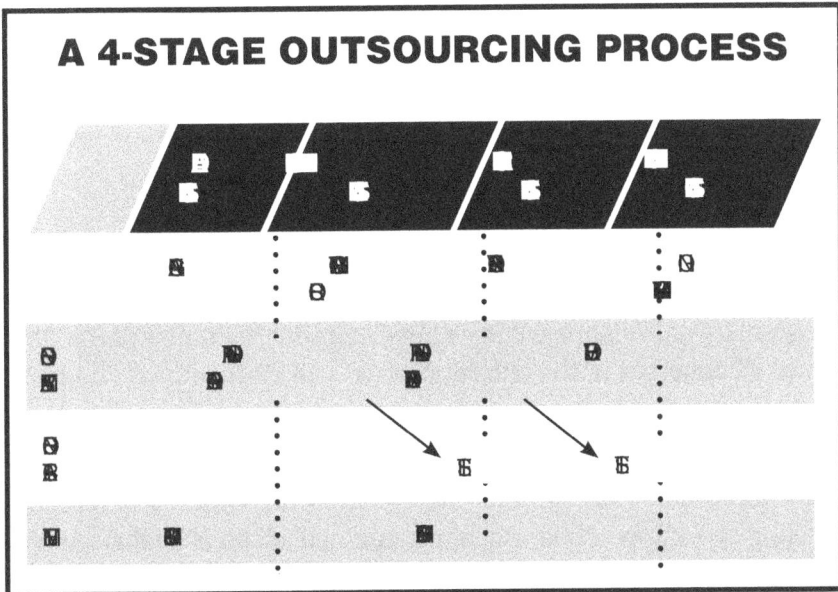

A 4-STAGE OUTSOURCING PROCESS

FOUR PHASES OF IMPLEMENTATION

We see the implementation process as four critical phases:

1. IDEA STAGE - Planning
2. IMPLEMENTATION STAGE - Migration of Processes
3. TRANSITION STAGE - Changeover
4. MANAGEMENT STAGE - Ongoing Improvement

1. Planning

The planning phase is the first step in implementing the outsourcing process. An experienced person in outsourcing is a vital resource in establishing a plan that will evolve into a successful outcome.

To begin, the provider and/or consultant needs to review the clients' back-office functions, needs, and requirements. Soon into the process, assessments must be made to be sure the IT system can support the accounting and other business processes that are to be

39

developed for outsourcing. If the system is obsolete, the client has to be willing to re-engineer and make appropriate upgrades. The provider can act as advisor and works with the existing management and IT department, if one exists. If there is no in-house IT personnel, experts can be brought in.

Secondly, the provider and/or consultant should present to prospective clients an initial snapshot of how their operations will function in an outsourced environment. At the same time, a preliminary cost estimate can be developed for the transition. At this point, weaknesses in the current process can be identified and fixed so they can be smoothly transitioned.

In the next phase of planning, extensive interviews are conducted with representatives in the organization in order to map the existing workflow. Next, an organizational chart is prepared. Not every business function is appropriate for outsourcing; therefore, recommendations must be made as to which functions should be outsourced and how this is to be accomplished. Additionally, an outline is developed on how processes are managed and how workflow can be more efficient.

Manufacturing company wants to streamline

Recently, a BPO provider met with a Miami-based manufacturer about outsourcing their entire back-office activities, such as processing accounts receivables and payables and doing bookkeeping to streamline their back-office processes. The goal was to develop an IT system for the accounting process, including account receivables, invoicing, CRM, account payables, bookkeeping and final financial statements. In addition, the goal included implementing a paperless office using a web based solution.

continued next page

40

Many of the business processes being administered are highly sophisticated. To automate the accounting activities, the provider obtains a preliminary time period and budget to achieve the goal. Before the project begins, a detailed flow chart will be developed to demonstrate how the business processes will work utilizing preferably web-based solutions. The benefits are endless: cost savings, the opportunity to re-invest the savings into the business, less work for the CEO and other employees. Lastly, when all is said and done, the value of the company will be increased exponentially.

Throughout the planning stage, the consultant recommends technology solutions, wherever and however required, and how they should be phased in. Talking to staff is extremely valuable to get a clear picture of what needs to be accomplished and then how it should be outsourced in the most efficient manner. The skill set required in the task to be outsourced should be defined.

When all of the key issues are agreed upon, especially the identification of functions to be outsourced, a contract is prepared, and upon agreement between both parties, the outsourcing process begins. Comprehensive testing is conducted, all according to a detailed workflow and an agreed upon work schedule.

2. Implementation

During the implementation phase, the provider and client members create a team to begin to work out the migration of processes. Together they review staffing issues and begin identifying process improvements, workflow enhancements, and technology upgrades. Technology solutions may include document imaging and web-enabled workflows, critical aspects of implementing the outsourcing solutions.

The success of the process will depend on this phase as each function is mapped out in detail. Mapping becomes the basis for transferring knowledge to the provider's staff, which will be carefully trained in the specific business process. One important note here in regard to knowledge transfer -- be conscious of achieving the right balance between transferring too little knowledge and too much knowledge. If too little knowledge is transferred, it can threaten the success of the outsourcing project. The provider needs to know all of the background details of the business process to avoid the possibility of making wrong assumptions and not meeting the company's needs.

Both the client organization and the provider must commit to sharing knowledge of the business operation. The joint team should engage in a series of discussions to clarify technical language and jargon that might be exclusive to the enterprise and its industry.

3. Transition

Once implementation has been laid out, the client and transition team starts the transition of specific processes that have been identified for outsourcing to the provider, which will supervise and perform those functions offshore and at U.S. locations. To ensure a smooth transition, specific plans are put into place for communication, workflow processes, technology, logistics and any additional training required. Workers can then be interviewed and trained by the BPO provider to produce the results desired. Metrics should be set up (SLA-Service Level Agreements) to monitor performance and to be certain each party understands the desired outcome and expected results. Metrics can define the acceptable time frame to perform the work, acceptable error rates, and collection ratios based on or exceeding industry statistics.

4. Management

Once the transition is complete, the client and provider continue to evaluate processes for improvement and operational efficiencies. On an as needed basis, the client and the provider communicate to evaluate best practices and discuss any snags in the process.

Throughout the outsourcing initiative, good communication is crucial. Bear in mind the fact that different cultures, time zones, and measurement systems are in play. For example, if the Maryland-based manager emails the team leader in Guatemala to set up a conference call, be exact since there is a one-hour time difference. Make sure that parties are identified and roles are defined so people can be held accountable. Emails should be succinct and to the point. They should not be overwritten or peppered with alarming words like **Urgent** or **High Priority**. These attention-getting commands should be used sparingly to avoid the "boy who cried wolf" effect.

In any relationship, good communication is the linchpin for success. Lack of the right language, or use of inappropriate or misleading words, can turn your best efforts into a failure in outsourcing.

"PODHURTZ HERE. OFFSHORE INVESTMENT CAPITAL, INC."

NINE

BPO Best Practices
Doing it right

The first rule of any technology used in a business is that automation applied to an efficient operation will magnify the efficiency. The second is that automation applied to an inefficient operation will magnify the inefficiency.

BILL GATES

In the preceding chapters, we have tried to explain in simple terms why outsourcing can make your business easier to manage, reduce labor and overhead costs, increase your net profit and the value of your business, and prevent business failure. If you want to continue to own your business, outsourcing can ensure future success. If you want to sell your company, outsourcing can favorably position you for acquisition. Remember, investors do not want to buy a company that is weighted down by heavy fixed costs. They are looking for flexible companies with strong core competencies.

To help you go forward on your journey to outsourcing, here are some industry best practices:

Best Practices: Ten No-Nonsense Pointers

1. Make outsourcing a crucial element of your strategic business plan
2. Outsource "non-core" and non-strategic processes
3. Retool and reinvent first -- don't outsource an inefficient flawed process
4. Hire qualified people to help negotiate and transition
5. Identify your stakeholders and communicate your plan clearly

45

6. Choose a provider with specific and relevant expertise

7. Negotiate a fair contract and governance;
   then commit to the relationship

8. Be flexible during the transition phase

9. Improve the process continuously

10. Set metrics and SLA to measure success
    or failure of the arrangement

What non-core activities are most successfully outsourced?

Accounting

- Invoicing
- Time and Expense Management
- Credit and Debt analysisent
- Collections
- Billing-dispute resolution
- Accounts Receivable
- Bookkeeping
- Accounts Payable Invoicing
- Financial Statements
- Bank Reconciliations

Human Resources

- Payroll
- Benefits Administration
- Training
- Contract-worker management

Supply management and procurement

- Procurement
- Logistics management
- Warehouse management

Customer Relationship Management

- Call center operations

Industry-specific processes
- Insurance claims processing
- Mortgage processing
- Check processing
- Health care-paperwork processing
- Data Processing

Selecting a Provider

When you are looking for a BPO provider, you want an organization that has experience in specific business processes, as noted above, relevant to your needs. Once you hire a BPO, think of it as hiring an employee. While you will be saving money, you still want to look for competence, not price.

A candidate's ability to generate results is the most important consideration. Above all, how well will they be able to provide the service? Is the service highly customized and personalized? Are there professionals available as often as you would like to address problems or issues? Do they have the ability to grow and develop with you? Do they have the technical capabilities to deliver?

THREE SUGGESTIONS TO BEAR IN MIND:

1. Hire with the idea of staying the course long term.
   You don't want to experiment. Consistency is important.

2. Hire specialists with the right expertise and potential.

3. Create a roadmap to start and improve the relationship at regular intervals.

4. Hold all parties accountable and identify the roles of management in the company, and at the BPO provider, to ensure communication is timely and high quality output results.

BPO providers are experts in running and managing these areas of a business!

"*More* outsourcing!"

TEN

Change Management
Top Down Transformation

*The world is more malleable than you think
and it's waiting for you to hammer it into shape.*

BONO

When change is proposed, it has to come from the top and over time sewn into the fabric of the company. The essence of any new system has to become part and parcel of the corporate culture. In much the same way that a new product or service is introduced and marketed to customers, an organizational change has to be promoted and sold to all of the stakeholders. Support for this paradigm shift can only come from the top!

In 1989, Jack Welch, then the chairman of General Electric, was visiting India and recognized the pool of talent there. He sent a group of executives over to check out the possibilities. Vivek Paul, now the president of Wipro, escorted the GE team around. Tom Friedman tells the story in *The World is Flat*. Five cars of GE people were touring around in Indian-made vehicles when they heard a loud bang and the lead car's hood flew off, smashing the windshield. Paul recalls, "I could just hear the GE people saying, 'This is the place we're going to get software from?'"

But Welch was a visionary and saw the potential. Today, GE's biggest research center outside the U.S. is in Bangalore, with about 1700 Indian engineers, designers, and scientists.

Successful changes in organizations always start at the top. The CEO is the Chief Architect of Change and has to direct the message and articulate it clearly so that it becomes part of the culture. In Broward County, Florida, the Parks and Recreation Department adopted a fitness program from the County School Board that taught the value

49

of exercise and good eating habits. The branded program *Commit 2B Fit* was incorporated into every level of the parks organizational structure, which required a massive marketing campaign to get the word out. All forms of marketing tools from logos and slogans to flyers to giveaways, events, and contests were utilized systematically to promote the fitness concept. The chief spokesperson for the fitness program was the Director of the parks systems. It was he who articulated the cause again and again to drive it through the organization and into the public consciousness.

Be patient, positive, and persistent

Outsourcing is not always perceived as a popular change. After all, many employees feel their jobs may be threatened. In fact, employees will quickly view it as a deskkiller. So it has to be introduced carefully and presented positively emphasizing the benefits to everyone. During the implementation process, employees are interviewed so that a workflow chart can be mapped out. This is a good time for employees to be kept informed so they will not feel threatened. They need to understand that outsourcing is being implemented to improve the company, not necessarily as a measure to eliminate their jobs.

Another way to present outsourcing is this: employees that perform tedious rote business tasks may become eligible for higher level jobs that are more critical to generating revenue, such as marketing and sales. Their talents and abilities can be used in other capacities that will have greater benefits for them and the parent company.

Change must begin with a highly respected individual in the organization. Usually it is the CEO or Chairman who has a demonstrated track record of foresight and accomplishment. A critical leadership skill is the desire to manage, not to do. In other words, the CEO or leader is the strategist and can imbue in others the vision and tools to roll out the program and get the work done.

The client organization and the outsourcing provider must be able to trust one another and feel comfortable working together. The provider must be reasonably free to control how the work gets done, while the client focuses on leveraging the results. If trust exists, then these characteristics will follow: consistency, fairness, sound decision-making, open communications, and a desire for everyone to succeed.

Communication can never be underestimated. Important ideas are hatched out of verbal and written communications; misunderstandings are dispelled. Clarity is achieved resulting in insights, innovation, and sound decision-making. A disciplined, consistent approach to examining each decision as to its potential consequences is needed. Through good communication patterns, the ultimate value of outsourcing is more quickly realized.

Handling Resistance to Change

Kris Taylor, an advisor to Vistage International, the world's largest CEO membership organization, was asked to consult about how companies can change their game plan, and not only survive, but thrive. She cites several ways CEOs can help staff welcome the change:

Ensure that people see why the desired end state is better than the present. When the change is perceived to be more desirable than the alternative, it is easier to accept. To make the case compelling, use hard numbers, stories, metaphors, and visual images to show how the change, albeit difficult, is positive for everyone.

Acknowledge mixed emotions. Expect ambivalence, involvement, negativity, enthusiasm, fear, eager anticipation, joy and sorrow, and lead your team through these undercurrents.

Be clear about what is expected from each employee and hold them accountable. Cast a broad net and get everyone involved in some way. Identify key leaders and give them a larger role.

Build in rituals and ceremonies to celebrate progress, provide recognition, and remember the past. Give mementos. Memorialize firsts: first dollar earned, first product created, first milestone achieved.

"Our salaries are so low, companies in India are
outsourcing to us."

ELEVEN

Contracts and Negotiation

Terms of endearment

***The secret of business is to know
something that nobody else knows.***

ARISTOTLE ONASSIS

The contract is intended to not only seal the deal, but to also establish a working framework for the outsourcing relationship. It should clearly define and describe the scope and nature of the initiative; roles and responsibilities of the client organization; roles and responsibilities of the provider; metrics for evaluating performance; and recourse if the relationship does not meet expectations.

Every contract binder consists of five elements:

1. A master contract
2. Operating principles
3. Metrics definition
4. SOWs
5. SLAs

One of the most important points to remember is that when you are structuring an agreement, you are negotiating a relationship rather than a contract. It is likely that the document will need some tweaking along the way and renegotiation. As with most relationships, it is difficult to foresee everything at the start. Once you are into the process, you will realize that certain changes have to be made. That's why it's best for there to be respect and trust between the parties so that adjustments can be made amicably.

Master Contract

In general, the master contract establishes the rules by which the client and provider will work together. It defines the intent of the relationship and how the parties will interact. It includes the financial terms of the agreement. Since every outsourcing arrangement is unique, the consultant has to be able to understand the most appropriate pricing model on which to put together the contract.

Statement of Work (SOW)

The Statement of Work (SOW) portion of the outsourcing contract should detail the scope of work, specifying the functions to be performed, the deliverables, and the roles of each party in the project. Be as detailed as you can to ensure that everyone involved clearly understands their responsibilities and the deliverables that are expected.

Service Level Agreement (SLA)

The SLA defines the parameters by which the work will be performed and judged. SLAs are attached to each specific SOW. Metrics will provide an accurate measure of performance.

Example: Data entry is the function. The metrics assigned to this task could be: Data updates are recorded by 5 p.m. each day. Review of new data occurs every morning between 9 a.m. and 10 a.m.

An effective contract should be comprehensive and clear. It should always include a realistic exit strategy. Lastly, avoid vendor-standard contracts.

Pricing Models

Time and material contracts work for short-term projects that are not necessarily recurring. They align with the temp agency model. It is when the vendor prices its services based on a predetermined negotiated hourly labor rate and charges back the actual costs for additional materials to the client. For example, if you outsource data entry for a given period of time, you are charged at an hourly rate or price per entry.

Cost-plus contracts are suitable for projects such as feasibility studies or research projects. These contracts are negotiated based on predetermined vendor profits guaranteed over the actual vendor costs. The vendor has no incentive to watch costs, so these contracts have to be closely managed.

Utility-based contracts are priced on a pay-as-you-go basis. They depend on the actual usage of the service by the clients, as in the usage of electricity. These contracts work well for short-term projects. For example, companies lease software applications or website hosting services on a pay-as-you-go rate.

Fixed-price contracts are when the vendor provides services based on the Statement of Work (SOW). A monthly fee, for example, is negotiated for the entire scope of services and is not contingent on the number of hours or workers. These contracts are used when requirements are clearly defined and mutually agreed upon by both client and provider.

Outsourcing Agreement Checklist

GENERAL TERMS

Have you included a statement setting forth the objectives, purpose and intent of the outsourcing arrangement in a manner that is an interpretive tool should there be any ambiguities within the agreement?

Have you stated the mechanism for renewal periods?

Have the permissible circumstances for early termination been clearly stated, and have you established the transition of personnel and equipment in the event of such early termination?

Scope of Services

Have you stated the scope of the services to be provided? If the agreement is complex, have you also included a representative list of possible ancillary services that may be needed, in an effort to minimize ambiguities?

Does the agreement cover the specifications for certain technology upgrades that will serve as the foundation of the outsourcing program?

Have you discussed and specified what key personnel will be trained to work on the project, and will be solely dedicated to this project in order to maintain a consistent level of knowledge and quality?

Does the agreement address any type of incentives such as gain sharing for BPO provider efficiencies and cost savings? Is it understood that such incentives may create cost uncertainty in the agreement and that clarification will be necessary?

Have you set goals for the service level that optimally can be reached, based on current industry practices?

Has the provider tried to set a cap on the level of service to be reached? If yes, do you think the provider's quality may be compromised once the cap is reached? This should be discussed.

Transfer of Assets

Have you stipulated whether or not the client will have the option of re-purchasing assets upon termination of the agreement? If the provider no longer has use for the assets, it would be in his best interest to have the client repurchase the assets.

Should repurchase of assets occur, it will be necessary for those assets to be inspected by the provider. Documentation will also have to be prepared. Is this process understood by both company and provider, since it can be time-onsuming and expensive?

In addition to transfer of assets, certain contracts and licenses may need to be transferred, and a due diligence review will have to be conducted to determine if these contracts are assignable. If they are not assignable, the party that holds the contracts will remain responsible for them. The provider and client may want to address this issue in the contract.

Fee Arrangements

The company's current in-house costs associated with the services to be outsourced should be carefully reviewed and analyzed, including both direct and indirect costs and overhead. Is the prospective outsourcing feasible and how does it compare to the provider's proposal?

Is the pricing model flexible and does it allow for the inevitable changes that will arise over the life of the agreement to increase or decrease personnel, etc.?

Benchmarking

Are the services priced competitively over the life of the agreement? Is the agreement automatically renewable and are conditions for untimely termination spelled out?

Is the provider making an investment in assets, such as software and hardware, to service the client? If yes, has the company considered that the provider is counting on a lengthy and steady stream of income to offset the initial investment? Who bears the cost of this investment?

Have metrics been defined so all parties are clear as to service level expectations?

Implementation and Administration

Has an implementation strategy been established to minimize the transition to outsourcing?

Is the agreement flexible enough to accommodate changes over the life of the project, due to advances in technology or adjustments in business operations?

Exit Strategies

Has a comprehensive and amenable exit strategy been negotiated to ensure the continued delivery of services with a minimum of disruption?

Has a fee schedule been considered during the exit transition?

Offshoring Issues

Does the company understand that some portion of the work will be outsourced to offshore BPO centers? Are they adverse to this arrangement in any way?

Are there any domestic laws that they are aware of in their industry, such as personal privacy laws, which would prohibit or inhibit the transfer of data and goods out of the domestic jurisdiction?

TWELVE

The Future of Business
A Virtual New World

Outsourcing is growing in scale…
but becoming more complex to manage
and requiring a new set of skills.

ERIC SORENSEN
President & CEO of Sun-Rype Products Ltd.

Looking into the future, business will continue to change. Will the virtual office become more widespread? Will the hierarchy in organizations continue to become a more diffuse structure? What will happen in technology to improve processes?

Whatever the future brings, it is likely that the role of outsourcing will continue, because it is one of the best ways to reduce overhead, increase productivity, and to free up time for senior managers to focus on strategic business divisions and revenue generation.

The issue is not about the future of outsourcing, but how to implement it and make it work smoothly and seamlessly for your business. We hope this book has pointed out some of the promises and pitfalls of outsourcing and how it can transform your business into a more innovative company. That kind of company is worth more to those in it, and to the stakeholders that invest in it.

Here's how we envision the innovative company of tomorrow:

- Fostering creativity through a diverse culture
- Mutual respect among the global workforce
- More virtual offices
- Global workforce

- Super quick, efficient organizations
- Vanishing hierarchy
- Ever-shifting network of suppliers and outsourcers
- Widespread use of technology tools to advance connectivity
- More flexible work schedules
- More comfortable work places
- Unique and more customized benefits

The landscape of business looks like this: increasing pressure to perform at peak levels, change from vertical organization to virtual organization, compressed investment cycles, rapid advancement in every aspect of business. All of these features make it critical to stay ahead of the pack, to constantly move forward, and to seek best-in-world expertise in every facet of the operation.

The classical structure of the self-sufficient organization is obsolete. The better approach is to focus their internal resources on the activities that make them money. Their core competencies -- the development of software, the manufacture of chip machines, the marketing of consumer products -- are what matters to maintain the competitive advantage. The remainder of the non-critical activities should be managed through outsourcing. The old business paradigms have vanished.

As the future unfolds, the organization creates interdependent relationships with specialized service providers for many of its critical functions that must be performed extremely well, but where the organization gains little competitive advantage by doing the work itself, according to IAOP. Businesses that refuse to change with the times will inevitably fail. Their margins will diminish until they can no longer afford to stay in business.

THIRTEEN

Industry Standards
Shaping the Future

As we look into the next century,
leaders will be those who empower others.

BILL GATES

The widespread use of outsourcing has actually spawned a new industry and a global membership-based organization called the International Association of Outsourcing Professionals (IAOP). It brings together leading companies involved in outsourcing as customers, providers, and advisors. There are over 250 organizations from around the world representing a cross-section of industries and functional activities. IAOP provides conferences, classes, and networking opportunities to educate companies towards the goal of establishing high standards for the professional, shaping the future of outsourcing as a management practice, as a profession, and as an industry.

The International Association of Outsourcing Professionals defines outsourcing as such: "Outsourcing is a long-term, results-oriented business relationship with a specialized services provider. The services contracted for (including manufacturing services) may encompass a single activity, a set of activities, or an entire end-to-end business process. In most cases, and especially for larger organizations, what's being outsourced was previously performed by the customer organization for itself and is being transferred to the provider. In other cases, however, these may be activities the customer organization never performed itself."

What is meant by "long-term?" Many outsourcing contracts are five, 10, or even 15 years in duration, but many can be cancelled on

30-days notice. The term long-term means that it is the company's intention to divest itself of the capacity to perform the work internally. The company has made a strategic decision to shift a certain business process to the marketplace of outsourcing providers. While a contract with one provider might not end up being long-term, the process is usually permanently outsourced.

The term "result-oriented" suggests that the provider is taking on the responsibility for the processes, technologies employed, and the people that will perform the tasks. The provider assumes responsibility for the best possible results. Responsibility for the results is what differentiates outsourcing from the traditional temp agency.

The responsibility factor places outsourcing in a unique position along the continuum of outside relationships common to most business operations. As shown in the diagram, relationships range from the traditional procurement of supplies to highly collaborative relationships, such as strategic alliances and joint ventures.

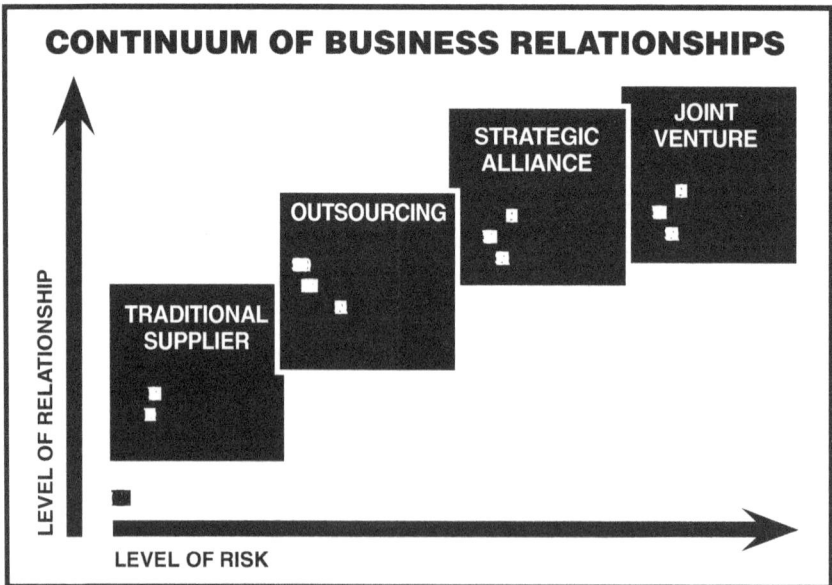

CONTINUUM OF BUSINESS RELATIONSHIPS

JOINT VENTURE

STRATEGIC ALLIANCE

OUTSOURCING

TRADITIONAL SUPPLIER

LEVEL OF RELATIONSHIP

LEVEL OF RISK

FOURTEEN

Life After Outsourcing - A Dramatization
Easy Living

*Intermission is an essential part of creating
a better circus performance.*

JONES LOFLIN and TODD MUSIG
Juggling Elephants

You did it. You made the transition to outsourcing. You have become the master of your fate.

We have here today a panel of CEOs that had the courage of their convictions to outsource their back-office business processes, including accounting and financial reporting. They based their decision to outsource on the need for efficiency, order and stability, and let's face it -- bigger profits.

Meet Perry Cavites, the CEO of Wizard Dentistry, Inc., a leading manufacturer of dental equipment; Richard Trumpet, owner of Big Note, a medium-sized retail chain specializing in musical instruments; and Sheila Tooley, CEO of a family-owned construction company that has operations in four states.

Question: How long did it take you to complete the transition to outsourcing?

Tooley: Once I made the decision to outsource our bookkeeping and accounting, it took the consultant about one month to assess our needs and plan the transition. The entire implementation from assessment to migration was six months.

Cavites: Our company was recently acquired by a publicly-held dental technology conglomerate and we were under intense pressure to squeeze more profits out of the business. Meanwhile our back office people were overwhelmed by the amount of paper work and data entry. It was a tremendous strain on me personally to cut costs and make sure everyone was being managed effectively. We completed the outsourcing process and migration in less than six months.

Trumpet: Everything was in place in about five months. We are looking to open more stores, so we knew that we had to deal with our valuation to obtain investment money. We had too many people doing the same back-office tasks, so there was a lot of redundancy in our operations. We were able to centralize and cut our overhead drastically.

Q: What does your new life look like now?

Tooley: For me, it has truly been a liberating experience. Before the outsourcing, I was tied to the office keeping a close eye on workers. Now I travel and visit my grandchildren whenever I want. We have a solid team in place in charge of new projects, work orders, inspections, and all of the tasks that go into administering construction projects.

Cavites: We completed the outsourcing, we were able to shift some of our workers into other positions, and we let go of about eight people who we felt were underperforming. With the accounting being done by experts, I have better data to see where we are headed. Our parent company is pleased to see we are in a solid growth mode where we can manage sales and inventory much better. Net profit is up and I get to spend more time on the golf course.

Trumpet: I'm writing my memoirs from my beach house. The transition to outsourcing is done and we are pleased with our provider. The key to success is trust and good communication, which is in place. Wherever I travel, I log in and see that the business is running smoothly. Accounting is updated daily and sales are increasing. I'm able to focus on our core business, adding products to our line, and getting more creative about merchandising in our stores.

Q: What have you learned from this experience?

Tooley: If my business is going to succeed and grow, then I have to be a good leader. Sometimes that means letting go of some things and delegating responsibility. This is why outsourcing is working for our company because we gave our non-core tasks to experts that can do the job better than we can and at half the cost. That's pretty darn good!

Cavites: Now that I have more free time, I think more clearly and have been able to set some new goals for the company that will add to our bottom line. As for me personally, my health has improved and I can sleep through the night without worrying about cash flow. Outsourcing is the best road I ever took.

Trumpet: I've learned that business is like a circus and I am the ringmaster. No one can juggle elephants, especially all at one time, as I recently read in the book *Juggling Elephants*. You can only be in one circus ring at a time and you have to set priorities in your business and your life. That means taking breaks and clearing your head, because a lot is riding on a CEO's ability to run the company and move it forward.

IMAGINE

Imagine a well-organized workplace with the most cutting-edge technology…

Imagine an accounting system that is updated daily… effortless billing and collecting accounts receivable with none of the headaches…

Imagine an office where nothing ever gets lost…

Imagine access to accurate and timely data at the touch of a button…

Imagine having experts manage all of your back-office processes while cutting costs up to 50%...

Imagine running your business with key indicators at your fingertips from anywhere in the world…

Imagine having real time access to statistical trends in your business and industry, monthly, so you can spot issues and resolve them before they become problems…

Imagine no more worries about cash flow fluctuations… without any surprises, because data gives you a clear picture of what's coming up…

Imagine tax planning throughout the year to save money on your taxes…

Imagine no more employee turnover disrupting business…

Imagine your company at the top of its game…

Imagine ever-increasing bottom line net profit and enhanced value.

In the 20th century it was called delegation and efficiency.

In the 21st century, it is called outsourcing.

Isn't it time to focus on your core business?

Glossary of Outsourcing Terms

Activity-Based Costing - Refers to the way a service is priced. Answers the questions: "How much does it cost to do that?" For example, how much does a company spend processing a receivable or taking a customer call? How much does it cost a city to repair a fence? The term relates to outsourcing in that once an organization can answer the cost questions at the activity level, it can more objectively compare the cost of internal versus external sourcing for performing it.

ASPs - Application Service Providers are companies that remotely host software applications and provide access to and use of the applications over the Internet or a private network. Almost all outsourcing service providers rely on the ASP model for linking aspects of their services to the customer organization.

Benchmarking - a study in which components of a company's contracted service, such as price, service levels, and terms and conditions, are compared to those of peer companies. An independent entity will usually conduct the study to provide a reasonably objective assessment of the performance of a specific service. Benchmarking is a continuous process whereby an enterprise measures and compares its functions, systems, and practices against strong competitors. The objective is to identify quality gaps in the organization and achieve a competitive advantage.

BPO - Business Process Outsourcing combines two powerful business tools - business process management and outsourcing. Business process management makes use of technology to break down barriers between traditional departments that are usually separate, such as finance and accounting, sales order processing, and call centers.

Many of these departments, though essential, are involved in non-critical activities. They do not make money for the company, yet the business cannot exist without them. Outsourcing employs the talent of specialized outside service providers to perform these critical, yet non-core activities. BPO examines a company's processes and determines which can be better performed through the outsourcing mechanism.

Captive Centers - Offshore facilities set up by companies to handle certain internal business functions and sell those same services to clients. For example, Microsoft, IBM, and General Electric have captive centers in India, some of which are call centers. Some companies, such as Motorola, have captive centers for research and development.

Change Management - Companies that institute organizational change take a systematic approach. It encompasses internal planning, initiating, managing, monitoring, and stabilizing change processes. Change may include strategic planning and direction or professional and personal development programs for staff.

Core Competencies - Unique internal capabilities and products that define a company's competitive advantage, as seen by its customers. The core competencies are the reason for the existence of the company. For example, Apple Computer designs and sells the Mac computer, the I-pod and I-phone. Microsoft develops computer software. Toyota manufactures automobiles. Proctor & Gamble develops and markets a huge array of household products. These are core competencies.

Critical versus Core - Many operations are critical to the business organization, but are not considered the reason for the company's existence. A classic example is payroll. Processing payroll accurately and timely is critical to the success of any organization and its employees, but is not actually a core competency.

Economies of Scale - A term used to describe the efficiencies of a service provider that can be achieved through standardization, commodity negotiation, and adherence to process management.

Exit Plan - A plan for easing out of an outsourcing contract. It involves the careful selection of a new provider that can implement a smooth transition to maintain service levels.

Innovation Capture - An organization wants to exploit new technologies that can improve business process. Sometimes, the service provider may be unwilling to invest unless the client pays. Contracts have to be structured to reward the service provider with a portion of savings won.

ISO 9000 Series of Standards - Series of standards established in the 1980s by Western Europe as a basis for judging the adequacy of the quality control systems of companies.

ISO 9001 - A quality assurance model from the International Organization for Standardization made up of 20 sets of quality system requirements. This model applies to organizations that design, develop, produce, install, and service products.

Labor Arbitrage - In outsourcing, the term is used to describe the savings an organization derives when it goes to lower wage labor markets, usually offshore.

Multinational Corporations - Usually this refers to companies that maintain captive centers in many countries. They are able to serve a global market of clients and tap the labor arbitrage because they are offshoring specific business functions, such as IT services, finance and accounting, and human resources. Examples of companies are IBM, HP, EDS, Accenture, and Keane.

Nearshore Outsourcing - When a company shifts work to service providers or companies in a nearby country, usually one that is close by or shares a border with its own country, such as Mexico or Canada. One of the benefits of nearshoring is the time zone, which is the same or nearly the same.

Offshore Outsourcing - When a company shifts work to service providers or companies in other countries. Prime examples are India, China, and the Philippines where there are many customer call centers.

Outsourcing - The process of transferring a specific business process to an external service provider, which becomes responsible and accountable for those services.

Pricing and Payment Terms - In the outsourcing industry, commitments run back-to-back. This means that when a client commits to the provider, the provider makes a commitment to its resources. Several pricing models in the outsourcing industry are: fixed-price; time and material; or performance-based. There can also be combinations of these models.

Process Mapping - When a company makes the transition to outsourcing, the specific business process is mapped out, so that everyone involved understands how the process is organized and executed.

Sarbanes Oxley - Sarbanes Oxley requires that all processes be documented and evaluated periodically for compliance with accounting principles (GAAP, FASB, etc.) All processes can be audited for compliance and for that reason, outsourced processes have to be treated as any other in-house process. The provider, therefore, is usually required to follow the guidelines established by Sarbanes Oxley and the ethical standards followed within the organization.

Scope of Work - Scope of work (SOW) for any project is crucial and should be drafted with extreme attention to detail. The entire process and the work to be performed must be clearly defined.

Service Level Agreements - Service level agreements (SLA) should be made to ensure client and vendor expectations are clearly defined. Quality and delivery concerns are two important issues to address, as well as mutual agreement to the terms. Care should be taken to keep reasonable margins, as there is always a margin of error. A renewal clause written in to the SLA should help fine tune the process, as initial problems get ironed out.

Stakeholders - Any individual or organization that has a vested interest in a company or entity. Any stakeholder carries certain perceptions of the company and expectations of what can be achieved.

Value-added Outsourcing - When a specific business function is transferred to a service provider, enabling value to be added to the activity. The presumption is that the provider can perform the function more cost-effectively than the internal department or staff.